VALENTINES DAY JOKES FOR KIDS

1. What did the calculator say to her boyfriend on Valentine's Day?

a. "You can count on me."

2. What did the drum say to his girlfriend?

a. "My heart beats for you."

3. What did the toad say to her to her boyfriend on February 13th?

a. *"Don't froget, tomorrow is Valentine's Day."*

4. What do you give a snake on Valentine's Day?

a. *A hug and a hiss.*

5. **What did the lightbulb say to the lamp on Valentine's Day?**

a. *"I love you a watt."*

6. **Where does beef go to meet potential Valentines?**

a. *To the meatball.*

7. What did the envelope say to the stamp on Valentine's Day?

a. *"If you want to go places, stick to me."*

8. Why do noses like to celebrate Valentine's Day?

a. *Because they are so scent-imental.*

9. **What do you call it when you see two sparrows on Valentine's Day?**

a. *Love birds.*

10. **How did the hornet ask the other hornet out?**

a. *She said "Bee mine."*

11. **What did one bee call the other on Valentine's Day?**

a. *"Honey."*

12. **What did the wasp say to the other wasp on Valentine's Day?**

a. *"I love bee-ing with you."*

13. What is it called when a squirrel is in love with you?

a. *He's nuts about you.*

14. What did the octopus ask the other octopus on their way home from their Valentine's Day date?

a. *"Can I hold your hand, hand, hand, hand, hand, hand, hand?"*

15. What kind of flowers did the squirrel give another squirrel on Valentine's Day?

a. *Forget-me-nuts.*

16. What do you call two cats in a good relationship?

a. *Purr-fect for each other.*

17. **What did the rabbit say in his Valentine's Day card to his secret admirer?**

a. *"Somebunny love you!"*

18. **What the did the square say to the triangle that he liked?**

a. *"I think you're acute."*

19. Why did the police officer take his girlfriend to jail on Valentine's Day?

a. *Because she stole his heart.*

20. What did one whale say to her boyfriend on Valentine's Day?

a. *"Whale you be mine?"*

21. **What did the volcano's Valentine's Day card say?**

a. *"I lava you."*

22. **Why shouldn't you kiss someone on January 1st?**

a. *Because it's the first date!*

23. **What do you get a French cook for Valentine's Day?**

a. *A hug and a quiche.*

24. **What did the dog write in his Valentine's Day card?**

a. *"I love you, drooly."*

25.   What did the grizzly say to his girlfriend on Valentine's Day?

a.   "I love you beary much."

26.   What did the artist say to her boyfriend on Valentine's Day?

a.   "I love you with all my art."

27.   Why should you not go to the restaurant on the moon for Valentine's Day?

a.   Because it doesn't have a good atmosphere!

28.   What did the sheep say to his girlfriend on Valentine's Day?

a.   "I love ewe."

29.   What did the moon say to the sun on February 14th?

a.   "Happy Valenshine's Day!"

30.   What did the bee say the first time he saw her on Valentine's Day?

a.   "You are bee-utiful!"

31. Why do you put hearts on Valentines?

a. *Because stomachs would look kind of gross.*

32. What did the sheep say after her boyfriend told her he loved her?

a. *"I love you baaaaack."*

33. **What did the owl say after the other owl asked him out?**

a. *"Owl be yours."*

34. **How did the bat ask the other bat on a date?**

a. *"Let's hang out."*

35. What did the elephant's Valentine say?

a. *"I love you a ton."*

36. How did the sheep ask the other sheep out?

a. *"Wool you be mine?"*

37.   What is the most romantic British city?

a.   *Loverpool.*

38.   Why is an artichoke best vegetable to eat on Valentine's Day?

a.   *Because it has a heart.*

39. Why do angel love stories always have the best endings?

a. Because they live harpily ever after.

40. What did the tape say to the paper on Valentine's Day?

a. "I'm stuck on you."

41. **What should you give your floor on Valentine's Day?**

a. *Rugs and kisses.*

42. **What does a vampire call his Valentine's Day date?**

a. *His ghoulfriend.*

43. **Why did the tennis players hit it off the first time they met?**

a. *Because it was lob at first sight.*

44. **What do you call a date between vampires that goes very well?**

a. *Love at first bite.*

45. **What does Frankenstein send on February 14th?**

a. *Valensteins.*

46. **What did the string say to her boyfriend on February 14th?**

a. *"Happy Valentwine's Day!"*

47. What did the frog say to his girlfriend on February 14th?

a. *"Happy Valenslime's Day."*

48. What did Dracula say to his girlfriend on Valentine's Day?

a. *"How do I love thee? Let me Count the ways."*

49. **What do you give a farmer on Valentine's Day?**

a. *Hogs and kisses.*

50. **What do you give a bell on February 14th?**

a. *A Valenchime.*

51. How did the shirt in the closet ask the other shirt on a date?

a. *"Want to hang out?"*

52. What did the syrup say to the pancake on Valentine's Day?

a. *"I'm sweet you."*

53. **What should you give broccoli on Valentine's Day?**

a. *Cauliflowers.*

54. **What did Bambi say to his girlfriend on Valentine's Day?**

a. *You're a deer.*

55. **What should you give to a boot-lover on Valentine's Day?**

a. *Uggs and kisses.*

56. **What is the best fruit to eat on Valentine's Day?**

a. *Dates.*

57.   What do you do when you fall in love with a dinner roll?

a.   You get buttered up.

58.   What did the magnet say to his girlfriend on Valentine's Day?

a.   I'm attracted to you.

59. **Knock knock!!**

Who's there?
Jimmy.
Jimmy who?
Jimmy a kiss.

60. **Knock knock!!**

Who's there?
Atlas.
Atlas who?
Atlas, it's Valentine's Day.

61.   Knock knock!!

Who's there.
Olive.
Olive who?
Olive you!

62.   What do you call it when two oars fall in love?

a.   Row-mance.

63. **What do you call it when two fish get married?**

a. *Guppy love.*

64. **Knock knock!!**

Who's there?
Sherwood.
Sherwood who?
Sherwood like to go on a date some time.

65. Why did the man trip down the stairs on Valentine's Day?

a. Because he was falling in love.

66. What do you say to a mitten on Valentine's Day?

a. "I glove you."

67. **What did the rock say to the other rock on Valentine's Day?**

a. *"Be mine."*

68. **What did the cherry say to his girlfriend on Valentine's Day?**

a. *"I love you berry much."*

69. **What did the nose say to his neighbor on Valentine's Day?**

a.   *"Eye love you."*

70. **What did the needle say to the fabric on Valentine's Day?**

a.   *"I love you sew much!"*

71.   What did the car say to the other car on Valentine's Day?

a.   *"I love you a lot."*

72.   What did the grape's Valentine's Day card say?

a.   *"I love you a bunch!"*

73. **What did the cake say to the pie on Valentine's Day?**

a. *"I love you to pieces."*

74. **What did the zombie say to her boyfriend on Valentine's Day?**

a. *"I love you to death."*

75.   **What did the calendar do on Valentine's Day?**

a.   *It went on a date.*

76.   **What did the bird say to the other bird on Valentine's Day?**

a.   *"I dove you!"*

77. **What do you get a dog-lover on Valentine's Day?**

a. *Pugs and kisses.*

78. **How does Santa sign his Valentine?**

a. *X Ho X ho.*

79. What do you call it when you fall in love with a pushpin?

a. *A heart-a-tack.*

80. In what month does Bigfoot celebrate Valentine's Day?

a. *Februhairy.*

81. **What do you call two mugs on a date?**

a. *A cupple.*

82. **What do you call it when two bugs fall in love?**

a. *Romantick.*

83. **What do you call a long walk on Valentine's Day.**

a.   *Roamantic.*

84. **What do you call a Valentine's Day date in Italy?**

a.   *Rome-antic.*

85. **What does a hotel call his girlfriend?**

a. *"Suite-heart."*

86. **What do you call a burning mailbox in February?**

a. *Valentine charred.*

87.   What did the harbor call her boyfriend?

a.   *Bay.*

88.   What did the billiard ball say to his girlfriend?

a.   *You're cuet.*

89.   What do you call it when two stuffed animals have been going out for a long time?

a.   Going teddy.

90.   What does the ghost call her sweetheart?

a.   Boo.

91. Why did the hatchet go on a date with his girlfriend?

a. Because he axed her out.

92. How do you ask a number on a date?

a. "Want two go out?"

93. **What did the pond say to her boyfriend on Valentine's Day?**

a. *"I really lake you."*

94. **What did the bicycle's Valentine's Day card say?**

a. *"I wheely like you."*

95. Knock Knock !!

Who's there?
Pea's
Pea's who?
Pea's will you be my valentine!

96. Knock Knock!!
Who's there?
Witches
Witches who?
Witches the way to your heart?

97. Knock Knock!!

Who's there?
Justin
Justin who?
Justin time to be your valentine!

98. Knock Knock !!

Who's there?
I love
I love who?
Aww, I love who too!

99. Knock Knock!!

Who's there?
Ben
Ben who?
Ben waiting my whole life for someone like you!

100. Knock Knock!!

Who's there?
Cute
Cute who?
You

Made in the USA
Lexington, KY
12 February 2018